TIM TAXIS

Hot For Cold Calling in 45 Minutes

How to Boost Your Success Rate on the Phone

Taxis, Tim
Hot For Cold Calling in 45 Minutes : How to Boost Your Success Rate on the Phone

ISBN 978-3-00-047039-4

Marketing & Sales
1. Sales – Selling. 2. Sales – Cold Calling

Editor: Tim Taxis, c/o Tim Taxis Training
Mauerkircherstr. 94, 81925 Munich, Germany
www.tim-taxis-trainings.de/hot-for-cold-calling-book-speaker
www.timtaxis.com

Publisher: IngramSpark, Ingram Content Group Inc.
Printed and distributed by IngramSpark.

Layout, Typesetting, Production:
text-ur copywriting and public relations agency Dr. Gierke,
Cologne, Germany, www.text-ur.de

Translator: Christian Villano
Translation Editor: Esther Lenssen, lenssenmedia.com

For sales inquries (bulk/retail), please contact the publisher: www.ingramspark.com
For other questions, please contact Tim's agency at: info@text-ur.de

ISBN 978-3-00-047039-4

© 2015 by Tim Taxis
Originally published in German in 2012 as *Heiß auf Kaltakquise in 45 Minuten – Wie Sie das Vorzimmer erobern und den Entscheider gewinnen*

What This Practical Guide Can Do for You

Are you looking for more success on the phone and unique methods that truly work?

Then you've come to the right place!

This book has purposefully been written so concisely that you can read it in 45 minutes.

This guide will help you accomplish your goal in cold calling in a manner that is:

- genuine
- far easier
- thoroughly enjoyable
- highly successful

Regardless of whether you're a newcomer or an experienced prospector: You are guaranteed to find new, unique, and effective methods for your success on the phone.

I am certain of one thing: If you apply what you learn in this little book, you too will soon be "hot for cold calling!" That is my sincere wish for you.

Yours

Tim Taxis

tt@timtaxis.com

Table of Contents

1   **Jump Start: Real-Life Cold Calls**   **7**

2   **Get Rid of the Textbook!**   **14**
2.1   Why Traditional Cold Calling No Longer
       Works   14
2.2   How to Be Naturally Successful Nowadays   17
2.3   The Golden Thread in Cold Calling   19

3   **Your Preparation: What to Look Out For**   **23**
3.1   Where and Whom Are You Actually Calling?   23
3.2   Your Ideal Prospecting Workplace   28
3.3   How Making a Call Can Become a Genuine
       Pleasure   31

4   **Pass the Switchboard First, Then Persuade
       the Gatekeeper**   **42**
4.1   The Greeting: How to Win Over the Person
       on the Other End   42
4.2   The Switchboard: How to Elicit Names and
       Information   45
4.3   "What Is This Regarding?":
       How to Persuade the Gatekeeper   48
4.4   Special: The Answering Machine —
       Friend or Foe?   55

5   **How to Win Over the Decision Maker**   **60**

5.1   New and Effective Openers That Are
       Guaranteed to Work   61

5.2   Investigating the Customer's Needs:
       Persuasion Without Argumentation   69

5.3   Client-Centered Argumentation   80

5.4   "No Time, Not Interested, Please Send Us
       Your Details": How to Handle These
       Objections Skillfully   85

5.5   Closing: How to Get a Yes From Your Client   100

1

Jump Start:
Real-Life Cold Calls

To give you an immediate idea of how your future prospecting calls will unfold with the aid of the methods laid out in this book, we will begin with a few concrete examples.

Note that these examples use my personal wording. Please use your own phrasing in the future. That is to say, any time you come across a phrase in the book and think, "Wow, I like that," then go ahead and use it verbatim. If, on the other hand, you think, "Hmm, that's pretty good, but not really my style," then make the necessary changes to suit your personal choice of words. Authenticity is crucial.

In the following chapters we will look at individual segments of dialogue and their psychological motivations, step by step. Within 45 minutes, you will have all the tools necessary to make your cold calls as smooth and successful as the ones below. Let's get started:

Ramon Hernandez, the sales manager of a transport company, would like to target the wholesale firm Carter & Sons as a new customer and phones the head of logistics, Derek Baley, for the first time:

Switchboard: "Carter & Sons, this is Jeremy speaking, how may I help you?"

Hernandez: "Good morning, Jeremy, this is Ramon Hernandez from LogiSpeed. How are you doing?"

Switchboard: "Good morning."

Hernandez: "Please put me through to Derek Baley's personal assistant."

Switchboard: "One moment . . ."

Personal Assistant: "Martina Moore speaking."

Hernandez: "Good morning, Ms. Moore, it's Ramon Hernandez from LogiSpeed. How are you doing?"

PA: "Good morning."

Hernandez: "Say, is Derek Baley in yet?"

PA: "Yes, he is."

Hernandez: "Then please pass me to him, thanks."

PA: "Uh, alright, just a moment, please."

Too easy? Not realistic? Compare it with your own phrasing. The subtleties of this method lie in the psychological details underlying the formulations used — and we will take a closer look at them in the course of the book.

Now let's look at a slightly tougher approach:

PA: "Martina Moore."
Hernandez: "Good morning, Ms. Moore, this is Ramon Hernandez from LogiSpeed. How are you?"
PA: "Good morning."
Hernandez: "Say, Ms. Moore, is Derek Baley in yet?"
PA: "Yes, he is. What is this regarding?"
Hernandez: "It's regarding his logistics processes, in particular his freight shipments to Asia. Please put me through to him, thanks . . ."
PA: "Er, OK, one moment."

And if you're still thinking, "No, that's not realistic," then let's try the exact same conversation, but "ice cold" this time:
(. . .)
PA: "Yes, he's in. What is this regarding?"
Hernandez: "His logistics processes, in particular his freight shipments to Asia. Please put me through to him."
PA: "Does he know you?"
Hernandez: "That's why I'm calling: I need his decision as head of logistics regarding the freight shipments to Asia. Please pass him to me. Thank you."

PA: "Uh, yes, one moment please . . ."

With this approach you remain honest, charming, but in control. The first time you try it, you'll notice how easily and effectively you can attain your objective.

Let's continue our cold calling:

Head of Logistics: "Derek Baley speaking."

Hernandez: "Good morning, Mr. Baley, this is Ramon Hernandez with LogiSpeed. How are you doing?"

HL: "Good morning."

Hernandez: "Mr. Baley, may I get straight to the point?"

HL: "Of course."

Hernandez: "I'd like to meet with you personally to discuss the optimization of your Asian freight shipping—but only if it can be of benefit to you. That's why I have a quick question; is that OK?"

HL: "Well, alright, go ahead . . ."

Hernandez: "If you could name *one* thing in the area of Asian freight shipping that doesn't always run as smoothly as you would like, what would that be, off the top of your head?"

HL: "Well, there is the issue of the hubs. At times our partners have prolonged delivery times because everything runs through the big loading stations. This isn't ideal for us . . . "

Hernandez: "I understand. And what would you like to see done in concrete terms?"

HL: "Simple: faster times through decentralized processes!"

Hernandez: "That's precisely why I'm calling you today: With us as partners you will attain faster times through decentralized processes. What I propose is that you get an idea of what this would look like for your company — we can meet up next week. When is most convenient for you?"

HL: "Hmm, then let's make it early Tuesday morning, around 9."

(. . .)

If you look at this conversation once again and replay it quietly to yourself — what goes through your mind?

You're probably asking yourself: Can it be this easy?

The answer is: of course, without a doubt. Perhaps not always, but increasingly often with the methods in this book, provided that you try them out for yourself.

But still I hear you say the conversation is "too easy." So let's run through the same one again, but in the "ice cold" version:

Head of Logistics: "Derek Baley speaking."

Hernandez: "Good morning, Mr. Baley, this is Ramon Hernandez from LogiSpeed. How are you?"

HL: (says nothing)

Hernandez: "May I come straight to the point?"

HL: "What do you want?"

Hernandez: "We would like to become additional logistics partners for your Asian freight shipping — but only if you could benefit from it. That's why I have a quick . . ."

HL (interjects): "No, we already have our longstanding partners and are very satisfied with them. I'm not interested. Thank you."

Hernandez: "Alright, in that case I just have one *final* question, is that OK?"

HL: "Oh, for God's sake . . ."

Hernandez: "From your point of view, if you had to name *one* thing in the area of Asian freight shipping which you are not in the least happy with, what *one* thing would that be?"

HL: "Well, you logistics people seem to look out for your own interests more than the interests of your customer!"

Hernandez: "I see, well then be honest, what would you want from a logistics partner who is *firmly* focused on *your* needs?"

HL: "Well, I'm supposed to accept longer delivery times, because lately everything goes through the big loading stations. They claim it will save money, but I see nothing but prolonged delivery times."

Hernandez: "You're right, some do it that way — but we certainly don't. So what would you like to see happen, in concrete terms?"

HL: "That's easy: shorter delivery times through decentralized processes."

Hernandez: "Precisely, Mr. Baley, and that is why I'm calling: In the coming week I can show you how you would attain shorter delivery times through decentralized processes by working with us as partners, taking into account your concrete demands and our reference projects. When would you like to discuss your own vision with us; is next Friday good for you?"

HL: "No, I can only do it on Thursday at 9."

(. . .)

Bottom Line:

Cold calling can be a lot easier than most people think.

If we are willing to get rid of outdated approaches on the phone, we will find the customer reacting differently in turn. In this way cold calling becomes a lot simpler and more enjoyable, for you and your customer.

2
Get Rid of the Textbook!

Nobody likes cold calling. Why is that? The reason is simple: In cold calling we usually experience a lot more failure than success. And yet, it doesn't have to be this way—quite the contrary. You will soon be experiencing undreamed-of success on the phone. Judging by the experience of tens of thousands of people who have employed my methods, a success rate of between 20-50% has become possible. Think for a moment, what that could mean for your future . . .

2.1 Why Traditional Cold Calling No Longer Works

We are the ones responsible for the high rate of failure prevalent in cold calling up until now.

What do I mean by that?

We tend to do precisely that which leads to what we fear most: failure and rejection.

By employing outdated behavioral patterns and stale formulas, we are usually the ones who provoke resistance and rejection in the client.

Think about it for a moment: If someone were to call you up at the office, would you enjoy listening to the dreary traditional lines such as, "Good morning, my name is Vincent Allegro with Roberts Inc. We are a leading manufacturer of xyz, and I would like to yada yada . . ."? Or worse: "Hi, this is Vincent Allegro with Roberts Inc. May I have ten minutes of your time?"

Nobody wants to hear that anymore. But one way or another, that's what everyone we call ends up hearing. It has failure written all over it.

A little background information: We are not the only ones with patterns (in our communication). The clients, too, have their own set of patterns (in their perception). The upshot is that if we start in with an outdated textbook approach, we are triggering a rejection mode in the customer. She automatically thinks, "Someone trying to sell me something, not again!" — and what follows instantly is, "I have no time, I'm not interested, and I'm already set!" These are not "no's *per se*," they are so-called "no's of rejection." The client simply has no desire for that kind of prospecting conversation. She hasn't even listened to what it is we're selling. And that is why most cold calls are over before they've even begun.

Bottom Line:
Nowadays nobody likes being sold anything—for fear of being played for a fool. However, buying on one's own initiative—that's something everyone enjoys doing.

My advice: Stop selling—in the sense of overselling—and you'll be instantly more successful.

So what do I mean by that?

How exactly does "selling differently from all the rest" work?

Traditional Approach	TAXIS Method "Modern Selling"

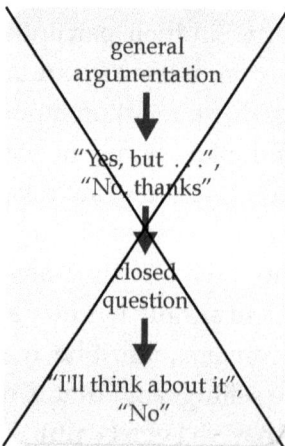

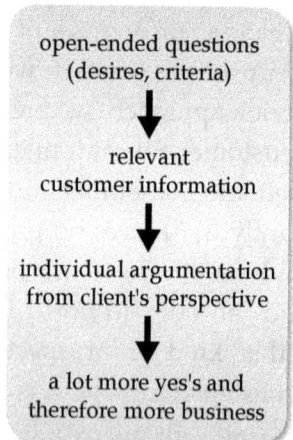

general argumentation

↓

"Yes, but . . .",
"No, thanks"

closed question

↓

"I'll think about it",
"No"

open-ended questions (desires, criteria)

↓

relevant customer information

↓

individual argumentation from client's perspective

↓

a lot more yes's and therefore more business

When you talk too much in the opening stages of a conversation, without putting questions to the customer, without engaging her actively in the exchange, without allowing her to talk and listening to her, you give her the impression that you're trying to con her into a purchase. And that is what people nowadays can't stand anymore. We are dealing with autonomous consumers, and so much the better. So the old textbook version is not going to work. What now?

2.2 How to Be Naturally Successful Nowadays

We simply need to replace the old patterns with new approaches — and we will automatically be successful. By altering your approach on the phone, you immediately alter the reaction that you get. Start your conversation with openers which do not trigger the rejection impulse. And above all, start replacing your statements with questions. Masters of prospecting are masters at asking questions — not at argumentation . . .

From now on, if *you* manage to shed your old behavioral patterns, step by step, and begin forging new paths, you will avoid triggering the rejection mechanism in your customer. The result? You'll see a maximal reduction of the "no's of rejection" and thereby unexpected success in your cold calling venture — and you'll have fun doing it! In the pages to come, we'll see exactly how this is done.

Building a relationship on the phone

Surely you've heard of phrases like "people make the business," or "business is nothing more than human relationships." How does this apply to cold calling? Easy: On either end of the phone is a person! And what does this apparently simple realization tell us? Even in their daily life at work, people want to enjoy themselves (personally) and conduct meaningful activities (business-wise).

Conclusion: Make sure that the person on the other end of the line finds the conversation enjoyable by creating a pleasant mood (the HOW = the relationship level). If you're able to communicate your concern so that the client understands that he will benefit from it (the WHAT = the business level), then you will be successful.

Bottom Line:

If you win over the person, you will win over the customer.

That is why building a relationship becomes paramount. The following considerations will help you reach the person on the other end of the phone:

- Prepare yourself in a professional manner.
- Do things differently from other prospectors: Get rid of old textbook formulas.

- Smile — the person you're speaking with will hear it.
- Greet your customer by name.
- Make sure to speak clearly and in a pleasant tone.
- When possible, seek out and use common points of interest.
- Show genuine interest: Ask questions and listen attentively.
- Give your client your undivided attention.

2.3 The Golden Thread in Cold Calling

Time and again I hear people say, "No, Mr. Taxis, there is no *single* recipe for cold calling!" Indeed, the *one*, sacred formula doesn't exist. However, all prospecting calls — as varied as they may be — share a common structure. It's like baking a cake: There are countless kinds of cake and as many recipes involved. Yet they all share a specific, structured procedure. Regardless of the type of cake you're baking and which recipe you're about to use, to make a cake the yeast or baking powder always goes into the dough before it all goes into the oven. Similarly, in cold calling there are certain steps that come before others, for example the greeting always comes before the opener. There is a common thread underlying every conversation:

The Golden Thread in Cold Calling

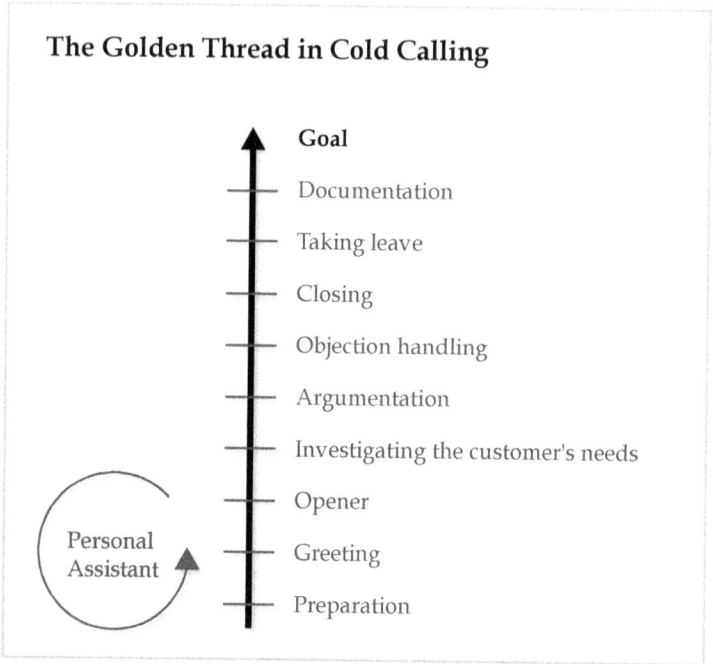

Goal

Documentation

Taking leave

Closing

Objection handling

Argumentation

Investigating the customer's needs

Opener

Personal Assistant

Greeting

Preparation

Of course it can happen that a client's objections arise earlier than indicated in the figure above. At times they come up directly after the opener. So, although there are deviations here and there, there is a fundamental structure underlying all of these types of conversation.

The layout of this book, then, follows this underlying structure. We will address each phase, step by step, and see the individual elements as strung together seamlessly, like pearls on a necklace.

It is imperative to learn this basic structure, and use it to your advantage:

By means of targeted conversation techniques you come to know what the customer is going to do next, or what options he has — and how to be prepared in dealing with them. The best prospectors approach their craft as a chess player would: They know the rules (the structure of the conversation), they know what options they have in a specific position (situation) and which possible reactions the other party will have in turn. And they always plan one move (step) ahead. In short, they know what's in store and how they must react most effectively in order to be successful.

Summary:

- Those who employ old sales platitudes provoke the rejection of the customer.
- Those who break old patterns in their own communication and forge new ground, will be highly successful.
- Show genuine interest in the person you're dealing with, for if you win over the person, you will win over the customer.
- Do not rely solely on your experience or your flexibility: Cold calls are not an "adventure," rather, they consistently follow the same structure. That is what you can and should prepare yourself for.

3

Your Preparation: What to Look Out For

Closing successfully depends on preparing professionally. "As much as necessary, as little as possible" is the axiom to follow here.

3.1 Where and Whom Are You Actually Calling?

Please don't simply pick up the phone and make the call. First consider whom you are looking to have as a customer:

Your target group
Not every company is suited to you and your proposal.

To make your prospecting as efficient as possible, separate the wheat from the chaff beforehand and define your target group. By target group we mean all companies whose business model, requirements and needs correspond with what you have to offer. In order to define your target group, you can start with your own positioning: What do you stand for? What can you do better than others? What problems can you or your products or services help solve? Which companies do these points apply to and which ones can benefit from them?

Alternatively, you can study the industries and companies that already belong to your client list and draw your target group from there.

As soon as you've gained some clarity about what your target group is, draw up a comprehensive enough contact list so that you will have sufficient prospecting "fodder" for a while to come.

The target person
There can only be one target person for you: the decision maker.

Now the question is: Whom do I wish to speak with — meaning whom do I wish to meet personally? Consider for a moment: Whom do you usually contact in a company when prospecting? Whom do you usually ask to be put in contact with by the switchboard?

Most people would bank on someone in the company who holds a position comparable to their own, someone they consider to be their counterpart on the customer's side. A field sales professional, for instance, will often contact a buyer at the target company. A sales trainer will get in touch with human resources. Why? Because we're in the habit of doing so.

Habits, however, are not the decisive criteria when choosing a point of entry for prospecting.

In order to establish where our best point of entry or access is in the hierarchy of a company, let's examine what the internal decision-making process is on the client's side of the equation (taking, for example, a medium-sized business to whom I would like to sell a *"Hot for Cold Calling"* training seminar).

Please note that here we are not looking at our own sales process, but rather our potential customer's company and their internal decision-making process.

Target the place where decisions are made: the decision maker.

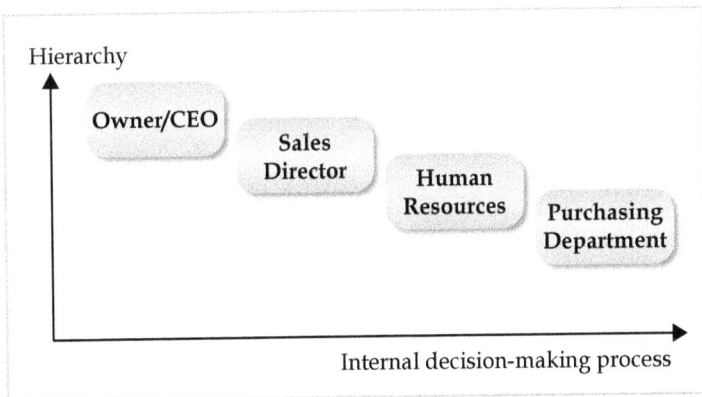

Hierarchy

Owner/CEO

Sales Director

Human Resources

Purchasing Department

Internal decision-making process

The heart of the customer's company lies at the very top of the chart: the decision maker. We define the "decision maker" as the person who alone can say yes to our proposal. This person presides over the budget and decides how the funds are allocated. Decision makers can have different titles and functions. They don't necessarily have to be on the executive board of a corporation or be the CEO of a firm. What counts is who provides the budget for your proposal. It is vital to determine who this is in every company you are dealing with.

Our initial contact will be the company's switchboard. Or — even better — the sales department.

Many sales professionals ask the switchboard operator who is responsible for this or that decision. Oftentimes, however, the operator is not privy or permitted to give out this kind of information. That's why I always call the department with the friendliest employees, who are often very well connected within their company and open to conversation: the sales department. Needless to say, the switchboard operator will always put you through to sales, and that's where you'll find the most accessible people and reliable information.

There are only good reasons for targeting the decision maker:

With anybody else you speak to, their decision will depend on the budget — with the decision maker, the budget depends on their decision.

. . . and that is certainly not the case in purchasing or with an employee in the respective department . . .

Therefore, locate the decision maker and look forward to speaking with her!

Individual preparation
Before you pick up the phone and dial your first number, get a hold of some more information that will be relevant to your prospecting success. The following points can be helpful:
- Business model and industry of the company
- Latest industry trends
- Latest company news
- Crucial access points into the business
- Organizational structure and locations
- Internal decision-making process
- Your own references in the client's industry
- Your history with the company, if you have one
- Information about the target person, the decision maker
- Common ground (with the company and/or the target person)

Please keep in mind: As much preparation as necessary, and as little preparation as possible.

If you are active in the B2B bulk business, then one or two minutes of preparation per company will usually be sufficient. If the complex B2B field is your area of business and you would like to prospect for individual, large-scale projects, then an hour of preparation per firm will be reasonable. You don't need any more than that. Otherwise you'll get swamped in what I call "shadow prospecting activities." After all, it makes you feel good to spend hours in prospecting preparation—you feel like you're "doing something." But for a successful initial contact on the phone, this kind of effort is simply not necessary . . .

3.2 Your Ideal Prospecting Workplace

An ideal prospecting environment makes your job easier. This applies to the following aspects:

Telephone

It is best to work with a headset or an earpiece (wired or wireless; for desk phones they are available at low prices). With both hands free it is simply easier to take notes during the call.

When calling, make sure to display your caller ID, as doing so indicates that you have nothing to hide.

As long as you're prospecting, let a colleague take your incoming calls and turn your cell phone off.

Writing material

Take notes longhand. Make sure you have a pad and working pen ready to hand.

Agenda
Make sure you have your agenda open, so that you can propose appointments without hesitation.

Computer screen
Always have your client's homepage open in front of you. A quick glance during the call can help you seize upon an important term or reference. Personally, I always find a photo of the target person on the Internet (via LinkedIn, Facebook or Google image search) in order to "look him in the eyes" while I'm calling. It lends a more personal, familiar air to the situation. Try it.

Script
There is no more hotly debated question in prospecting than whether or not to use a script.

Let's first clarify what it is we mean by script, so that we're talking about the same thing. When I ask my seminar participants what they make of the term "script," they usually say, "Oh, the thing they use at a call center. You can tell right away that they're reading it off the page. I don't want to come across like that. And if you ask them a question that's *not* in the script, they're at a loss for words. No, that's not my style." Do you have a similar opinion of scripts?

My personal view is that I do not want to come across as a person reading off a page when I'm on the phone. I want to be flexible. And that is precisely why I always phone with a script!

Granted, at the outset of my sales career I saw every prospecting call as an adventure. I would say to myself, "I never know what's coming, so I'll be flexible and wing it somehow." Today, however, I know that like every other person I am wired with certain behavioral patterns and cannot be flexible when it comes to trying out new things. I've also realized that cold calling is not an adventure, but a structured process that I can plan for. There are very few variations in this process, and these in turn follow the same structures.

The moment you realize this, your job will be much more effective, because there will be predictable situations arising which your script can prepare you for, so that you will invariably know what comes next.

Therefore you should always work with a script. Regardless of whether you apply it verbatim for every call, or whether it is detailed or a rough sketch: The moment you are in danger of losing the thread at a critical point of the cold call, it is good to know that you have it handy.

Miscellanea
It might be a checklist (e.g. your own product information), an evaluation form for your performance or a voice recorder (where legally admissible).

That's it
Anything that may distract or disturb you for the time that you're prospecting has no business in your workplace.

3.3 How Making a Call Can Become a Genuine Pleasure

So, now that everything "external" (your workplace) has been streamlined for prospecting, it's time to prepare the "internal" side—for as you surely know: Success lies between the ears.

The initial phone contact is something that many people associate with a variety of emotions, it's just that they're not good emotions. If that is how you happen to feel, then you can breathe easier because we're about to change it. Before long you'll be actually looking forward to reaching for the phone on a daily basis or whenever it is necessary for you to do so, to get in touch with potential customers.

What you get out of each dialing attempt
Most people see the innumerable dialing attempts which often end up failing to reach the right person as tiresome, and allow themselves to get frustrated by them. And yet, it doesn't have to be this way. Here are my thoughts on the matter:

At one time, many years ago in my first sales job, I made a few calculations: On average I had to dial 7 times to get 1 decision maker on the phone; out of 10 decision makers I was able to get 1 appointment. From every other appointment I got 1 inquiry and submitted 1 proposal. Out of every 3 proposals I got 1 order with an average value of $15,000.

Let's break that down: $15,000 divided by 3 (proposals necessary for one order) = $5,000, divided by 2 (appointments needed for one proposal) = $2,500, divided by 10 (calls needed for each appointment) = $250, divided by 7 (dialing attempts for each contact with a decision maker) = $35.71. That means that each time I picked up the phone — regardless of the outcome! — I made $35.71.

It's a good thing I figured that out because suddenly I was glad for every call I made. And that's what I kept in mind every time I thought about prospecting. I even found myself dialing one more time rather than one less at the end of the day.

I'd like you to take the time and calculate how much each dial of the phone is earning you.

Every time you pick up the phone — regardless of the result — you've earned yourself $xxx (xxx stands for the individual value which you have just calculated). So what do you say to that? Doesn't that put you in the mood for cold calling?

In case you're not too impressed with your present tally, try phoning companies that have a greater sales potential than those you have been calling up until now. The individual effort involved in the call remains the same — only the yield is greater. The numbers suddenly look better. And if you were to use the calling techniques provided by this book, you will increase your conversion rates and your individual value per call will rise accordingly.

How to handle a no
Every no is a learning experience – provided you use it!

At the start of my career, in my first sales job, my performance-based remuneration was at 50% of my compensation. Unfortunately, at the time I had no clue about sales, let alone prospecting. And this was plainly reflected in my results. I can tell you that if you're not successful, then a 50% commission feels pretty lousy . . .

After just twelve months, however, I was the best sales professional in my company in terms of revenue. My sales manager approached me one morning, stood with arms crossed and asked, "Tim, what is the secret of your success?"

Then, as now, I am firmly convinced that I am no different to all other salespeople. Except in one aspect. And this one aspect makes all the difference. Hopefully not for much longer, because here is "the secret of my success" for you: Out of necessity I began doing something which then became so natural for me that it never dawned on me that it might be what has set me apart from all the others to this day:

I reflected on my actions.

In other words, after every prospecting call and following every appointment in the field, I deliberately asked and answered the following questions:

How did it go? Did I attain my goal or not?

Success is always the attainment of pre-set goals — and in cold calling, whose goal is making an appointment with a qualified prospect, it is easily assessed: Either the appointment is made or it isn't.

On what did the outcome of the situation hinge?

In my experience, for every prospecting phone call there is a "key," a "pivotal point." And it is this point which you must deliberately pin down as you look back on it.

What did I say or do exactly?

Your precise analysis will help you endlessly in recognizing your strengths and making your room for improvement transparent.

How should I go about it the next time around?

That's what it comes down to from now on! We often do things without being conscious of them — even when they bring success . . .

Thus, if my actions were successful, I noted down in my script exactly what I did in a given situation, in order to have it ready for similar situations which would arise in the future.

If my actions were not successful, I thought about and wrote down immediately after the call—while the impressions were still fresh—how I could improve next time given a similar situation.

Bottom line:
Apply your strengths and improvements directly to your script. Make it a habit: Reflect on EVERY cold call.

Because if you manage to look back on every important situation and reflect on your actions and the effect they exert, then you will improve steadily and naturally.

A no from a customer can therefore be helpful and constructive—if you remain open-minded, if you wish to continually better yourself and if you reflect on your actions. Every no is a learning opportunity, which from now on you should begin to use systematically to your own advantage.

Another helpful consideration when handling a no
There is another insight which I garnered from my first sales job: As my success rate stood at 10%—1 appointment for every 10 contacts with a decision

maker—I realized that a no is nothing more than a link to the next yes. Statistically, the practical assessment of my performance had established that I only had to be well-prepared for and speak to ten decision makers, in order to be successful once. This gave me an almost exhilarating sensation. Why?

Before this realization, I used to go to work, suffer my first five no's, and then I'd give up, frustrated, muttering excuses like "not my day," "no luck," "wearing the wrong suit," —I'm sure you're familiar with this . . .

Once I understood that I effectively needed the nine no's in order to earn my next yes, it was nothing less than an epiphany. From then on I would walk into the office in the morning, get my first five or six no's—and I would sense a joy slowly but surely welling up in me. In view of my 10% success rate, I would think, "I have most of the no's behind me already, so my next yes must be just around the corner." Do you see what I mean?

How to Handle a No

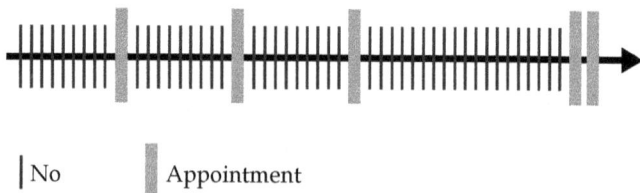

| No |▌ Appointment

And when I got 18 no's in a row — once reason enough for total resignation — armed with my new perspective I could hardly wait to keep on prospecting. My success rate was, after all, at 10% — and given that I had just received 18 no's in a row, I was due a marvelous double hit at any moment. The yes — statistically reliable — was about to come in twice. Alone this fresh perspective on an old predicament recast my inner attitude and turned my fortune around. It wasn't the predicament that had changed, it was my perspective on it that had shifted.

Apply these thoughts to yourself and let yourself be inspired!

This shift in perspective gave me a powerful sense of autonomy, which has lasted to this day. It helped boost my success rate to 50% within just a few years.

Additional tips for success

Are you hot for cold calling yet? In case a few more mental jump starts could be of use to you, I'll be glad to oblige.

How to make the first step an easy one

Granted, at times picking up the phone isn't so easy — especially at the outset of your prospecting career. So take the pressure off yourself, and put your mind at ease here and now with the following statement (feel free to say these lines aloud): "I will allow myself to make these first ten cold calls just like that, without expectation, regardless of what the outcome is. Whatever comes is OK with me. Here we go."

On either end of the line is a person

One of the most crucial realizations is as commonplace as it is (unconsciously) new for many people, and that is the fact that on either end of the line, there is a person.

If two people are communicating over the phone in a prospecting situation, the customer should not be seen as a "naysayer," a "rejecter," or a "gatekeeper from hell." But simply, an ordinary person. Like you and me.

If, on the other hand, you (even unconsciously) see the gatekeeper from hell, then you begin to put on your mental armor, and it is with this cumbersome protection that you charge into the cold war . . . I mean . . . the cold call. The poor personal assistant will immediately sense that you're armed to the teeth and will instantly switch into defense mode, or worse, into attack mode, herself. So let's put an end to this delusion. You're not in a spy thriller, you're just prospecting!

Speak to the other party as people, just as you would to your existing clients, whom you know and like.

Anticipate mentally the result you desire

You're probably familiar with expressions like "visualizing reality" or "self-fulfilling prophecy." What do they actually mean? By means of our thoughts, we anticipate a subsequent result and thereby exert an influence on it in advance. Both in positive and negative ways. Many people go (unconsciously) into prospecting with negative expectations. The result? Rejection.

Make sure you reverse this mechanism in the future.

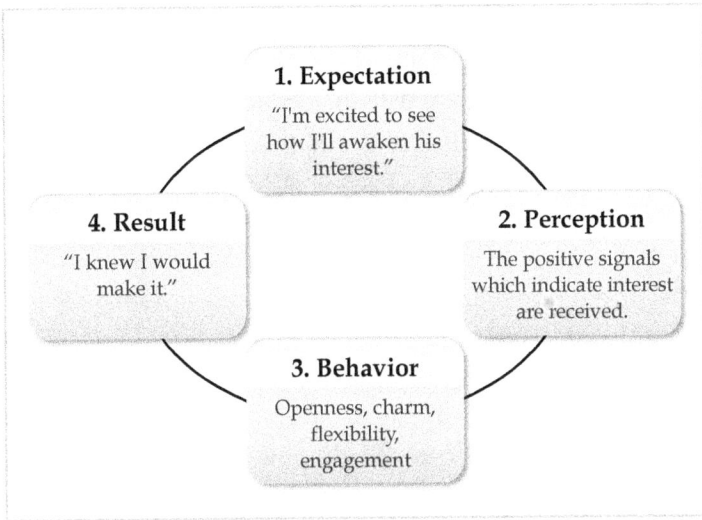

1. Expectation

"I'm excited to see how I'll awaken his interest."

4. Result

"I knew I would make it."

2. Perception

The positive signals which indicate interest are received.

3. Behavior

Openness, charm, flexibility, engagement

Bottom line:
The only thing standing in the way of your firm conviction that you can be successful in cold calling is the thought which claims the opposite.

You, however, have power over your thoughts, so become aware of this power. You will thank yourself for it later.

Your unconscious mind supports you in this: It filters all those signals from the conversation which concur with your attitude and expectation—and leaves all the rest out.

You're probably familiar with this filter from other situations: Have you purchased a car in the last few years? Which model was it? From the moment you became interested in this particular model, did you not begin to see it popping up on every street?

These cars were always there, you just didn't notice them. That's how our unconscious mind works.

Apply your mental focus on your desired result and use this effective principle deliberately from now on to ensure your prospecting success:

For example, before every call say consciously to yourself, "I want this appointment and I'm excited to see how I get the customer's interest. I've got nothing to lose, therefore I can only win. Here we go!"

Summary:

- Start your prospecting at a position in the target company where decisions are bound to be made, namely with the decision maker.
- Prepare yourself professionally.
- Preparation not only involves the "external" (your workplace), but above all the "internal."
- During a cold call, you project what is in you at that moment. If, for instance, you're feeling insecure and nervous, then this will in turn unsettle the client.
- Thus, before every call, do everything you can to put yourself in that state of mind which will help you in your prospecting venture.
- Reflect on your actions after every cold call. In doing so you will naturally continue to improve and be ever more successful.

4

Pass the Switchboard First, Then Persuade the Gatekeeper

So now the moment has come in which you reach for the phone after having prepared yourself thoroughly. If you follow the steps outlined below, you will be put through to the decision maker in situations in which you have failed to do so up until now.

4.1 The Greeting: How to Win Over the Person on the Other End

By "greeting" we simply mean your introduction, in which you give your name and your company's name.

Naturally, here too, there is a specific greeting structure which works better than others.

Please remember that the person on the other end of the line at any given moment is ALWAYS the most important.

This rule also applies to the switchboard or the PA. Why? Because whomever it is you're talking to will determine if and how your call progresses.

First, make sure you know what awaits you: The customer is at her desk, her head filled with all manner of things that need to be dealt with—except, of course, your phone call. Therefore, give the prospect the chance to react to you and settle into the conversation.

Imagine you are the one receiving a call and don't quite understand what the caller is talking about. How would you feel? Not very comfortable. That is why it is vital that you speak slowly and clearly, in order to be well understood.

I recommend the following greeting structure:

Greeting, customer's name, connecting phrase, your first and last name, your company's name, second greeting, pause:

"Good morning, Mr. Client, this is Ramon Hernandez from LogiSpeed. How are you doing?" Then deliberately leave a pause which your client can use to return your greeting. In this way an immediate exchange is established within seconds.

This is a crucial point, because most prospectors greet the customer and launch straight into their speech without pausing, and the customer gets the immediate impression that it's all scripted. Remember also to use the client's name in your greeting. This shows respect and gets his immediate attention.

Do not underestimate the importance of the greeting. It lays the foundation for the subsequent course of the conversation, either prompting the thought, "Who is this character?" or granting you the undivided attention you are seeking.

It is important to avoid fillers like, "*Yes*, good morning, Mr. . . ." or "*Uh*, good morning, Ms. . . ." or an overly effusive "salesmanlike" greeting such as, "Good morning, how are you today, Mr. . . ."

These approaches tend to lead to rejection. Make sure to speak in a clear, measured, friendly tone when using the structure outlined above, and you will have laid the foundation for a positive, successful exchange in the first few seconds.

4.2 The Switchboard: How to Elicit Names and Information

At the switchboard there are two basic scenarios: You either know the name of your prospect, or you don't. If you do know their name, then the next step is pretty straightforward:

You: "Good morning, Mr. Switchboard, this is Ramon Hernandez from LogiSpeed. How are you doing?" Pause.

Switchboard: "Good morning."

You: "(Mr. Switchboard,) please put me through to Derek Baley (your head of logistics), thank you."

Or,

You: "(Mr. Switchboard,) please put me through to Mr. Baley's personal assistant, thank you."

Or perhaps you don't know your prospect's name yet? Maybe as in many industries your prospect is the head of a specific department:

You: "Good morning, Mr. Switchboard, this is Ramon Hernandez from LogiSpeed. How are you?" Pause.

Switchboard: "Good morning."

You: "Good morning. Perhaps you could help me out, what is the name of your head of logistics again?"

Please do not ask, "Who is responsible for . . ." or "Whom would I talk to for matters concerning . . .?" These are old, hapless sales formulations that no one hears anymore. Moreover, with phrases like these you will not even reach the decision maker, but more often than not an employee from the respective department, or worse, the purchasing department. And in most cases, that's the last place you want to end up!

If in your industry your prospect cannot be readily assigned to a specific role or department, then the following script can help you:

You: "(Mr. Switchboard,) could you kindly tell me who in your company makes decisions on (your subject)?"

If the switchboard should not have this information or not be willing to give it out, try to reach — whenever possible — a department head who you think is most relevant to your mission, based on your experience.

Regardless of which approach you end up choosing, hopefully you will have gotten a name by now:

Switchboard: "That would be Mr. Baley."

Now what you want to do is establish what his first name is, which you will need when dealing with his personal assistant. For this there are two approaches. There's the direct approach, "What is Mr. Baley's first name?," though this might come across as a little intrusive. That's why this second alternative is much more effective:

You: "Oh . . . you mean Tom Baley?"
Switchboard: "No, Derek, Derek Baley."

By prompting the switchboard operator with a random name, you automatically trigger the response impulse, giving you the correct name.

If you want to obtain the direct extension number, then a direct question containing the word "extension" will frequently trigger an "I cannot give out that information" impulse. A better option is the following:

You: "In case he's not in, how can I reach him directly?"

Or,

You: "In case we should get cut off, how can I get back in touch with him directly?"

Then remain in control of the conversation by ending with:

You: "Great, I appreciate it, could you please put me through to him, thank you."

Now recall for a moment chapter 3.1. Oftentimes, the switchboard operator does not know or is not permitted to divulge the information we are after. That is why I always call the department which often boasts the friendliest, most talkative and best connected people in a company: the sales department. Moreover, the switchboard is sure to put you through to sales every time. Sales professionals are usually accessible and will provide you with the most reliable information. From there you can find your way to the decision maker, or, having at least obtained the decision maker's name, you can go back to the switchboard and proceed as outlined in the opening of this chapter.

4.3 "What is This Regarding?": How to Persuade the Gatekeeper

Frequently you will encounter a person who stands between you and the decision maker: the personal assistant. In most cases this will be a woman, therefore I will be using the female gender in the following pages.

The rules of prospecting apply to the gatekeeper as well: It's all about how you lead the conversation!

Whenever you answer a question from the client or personal assistant, make sure you conclude your answer with a question in return to remain in control of the exchange.

There is no situation less pleasant for a prospector than having to deal with the gatekeeper. Why should that be? Let's think for a moment about who exactly we are facing here. A four-eyed monster? An evil sentry that will not give way to anyone? A Hydra of rejection? Nothing of the kind, of course. It is simply a person. Like you and me. A person with hopes and fears like anybody else. Therefore, approach this person as your equal. Overestimate neither the gatekeeper nor yourself.

How would you react if someone called you on the phone and you noticed that they were trying to sidestep you as swiftly as possible, or treated you with arrogance, or began behaving submissively?

The answer is simple: You would lose respect for the person instantly, and as a gatekeeper, you would most probably say no, am I right?

And what is even more important than what you say, is how you say it. That is, by speaking slowly, by using short and clear sentences and a warm tone of voice, you will come across as natural, engaging, and respectful. You will also set yourself apart in the eyes of the personal assistant and win her approval.

The question "What is this regarding?" can have two purposes:

A request for factual information

Before a call is passed to the decision maker, usually that decision maker wants to know who is calling and what the call is regarding, therefore the intent here is purely informative.

Assessing factual information

Usually the PA is there to filter, to separate the important from the unimportant information. In that case, the question "What is this regarding?" serves as an evaluative purpose.

Unfortunately, we cannot always tell with certainty which purpose the question is serving. Thus, in order to reach the decision maker regardless of the question's intention, your answer should satisfy them both.

So, before you begin your call, think for a moment about what you ordinarily say when confronted with the personal assistant. How exactly does your script read?

This is the procedure I recommend:

You: "Good morning, Ms. Gatekeeper, this is Ramon Hernandez with LogiSpeed. How are you doing?" Pause.

PA: "Good morning."

You: "Is Derek Baley in already?"

Or,

You: "Say, Ms. Gatekeeper, is Derek Baley in already?"

This structure using first and last name plus the inquiry into the decision maker's whereabouts (". . . in already?") usually manages to quell the what-is-this-regarding impulse, and you will be put in touch with the decision maker.

With this line of questioning you give the impression of familiarity. That is the reason it works so well. As an alternative to "Is Derek Baley in already?" you can use any similar wording, such as, "Is Derek Baley still in his office?" or "Is Derek Baley done with his meeting?"

In this case it is important that you do not use the word "Mr." or the words "speak with." Both of these easily trigger the what-is-this-regarding impulse. If the answer is:

PA: "Yes, he's in."

then simply respond with:

You: "Then please pass me to him and tell him that it's Ramon Hernandez with LogiSpeed. Thank you."

If the answer is no then very naturally say:

You: "I thought so. When do you think he'd have two minutes to discuss (your field)?"

It's as easy as that.

Handling what-is-this-regarding questions

As good as this last approach works, in many cases you'll still have to deal with a "What is this regarding?" That means that you will have to prepare yourself for ways to handle this question. And here again, I will gladly repeat myself: Regardless of *what* you choose to say, it is *how* you say it that will be just as crucial.

"What is this regarding?" is the most natural question in the world for the gatekeeper, so there's no reason to get nervous about it. It is the PA's job to ask this question. And it is your job to be well prepared for it!

With the following three techniques you will significantly boost your breakthrough rate and reach the decision maker at a juncture where you may have failed in the past.

Select from the following:

Stating the obvious

The PA asks you, "What is this regarding?" and would like a short and sweet answer. However, given that she is used to hearing prospectors do the exact opposite—that is, launching into long-winded and fidgety explanations—you're going to give her exactly what she wants, clearly and with as few words as possible.

PA: "What is this regarding?"

You: "It's about his logistics processes, in particular his Asian freight shipping. Please put me through to him, thank you."

Don't prolong your explanation, otherwise you'll simply run the risk of sounding nervous and babbling, thereby promptly triggering the rejection switch. I call this the *stating-the-obvious technique* because you are expecting the question from the outset and providing a calculated and effective response.

If you should get a rare and unexpected rebuttal:

PA: "Does he know you?"

You: "That's why I'm calling: I need his decision as head of logistics on the matter of Asian freight shipping. Please pass him to me briefly. Thank you."

Using this technique you remain forthright, charming, and commanding. The very first time you try it, you'll notice how easily and effectively you attain your objective.

The preemptive approach

You can use this technique in harness with the *stating-the-obvious technique*. It is highly effective:

You: "Good morning, Ms. Gatekeeper, it's Ramon Hernandez with LogiSpeed. How are you?" Pause.

PA: "Good morning."

You: "Ms. Gatekeeper, I'm sure you would like to know the reason for my calling Derek (Baley) today before you put me through, am I right?"

PA: "Naturally."

And now simply proceed to employ the *stating-the-obvious technique*. Make sure to use a pleasant, understanding tone. The personal assistant will unconsciously be thinking, "Finally someone who understands my job." In this way you are putting her at ease. In addition, following her "yes" to your initial question, you are swaying her into an if-then condition: "If he gives me the reason for his call, I'll put him through."

This principle will ensure a considerably higher breakthrough rate.

The CEO–PA technique
This technique has proved successful at the highest levels of a company:

You: "Good morning, Ms. Gatekeeper, this is Ramon Hernandez from LogiSpeed. How are you doing?" Pause.

PA: "Good morning."

You: "Assuming I'm right in thinking that (first name and last name) is not available at the moment, I need your assistance, Ms. Gatekeeper."

PA: "How may I help you?"

You: "It's about our strategic collaboration in Asian freight shipping. Considering that she is the CEO, I would like to meet with her personally — but only if we can both benefit from it. I would need to consult her on this briefly over the phone first, it'll only take two minutes. Could you please check her agenda? When would be a good time to call her next week?"

Or,

You: "It's about our strategic collaboration in Asian freight shipping. I would need her decision on this as CEO in a brief phone call. When would it suit her for two minutes next week?"

Use words like "strategic," "political," "decision," "inquiry," etc. These are signal words which work wonders at this level. You may not so easily get a face-to-face meeting with a high-level decision maker, but you will likely get a phone appointment.

Approach your conversations with the gatekeeper with an open mind and enthusiasm. You will see that if you are pleasant and to the point with the PA, this aspect of prospecting will no longer be a liability but an asset.

Bottom line:
See the gatekeepers for who they are: people like you and me. If you replace the outworn communication patterns, you will set yourself refreshingly apart from all other prospectors — and you'll be naturally and effortlessly more successful.

4.4 Special: The Answering Machine — Friend or Foe?

You know the situation: In many cases, you don't reach your desired prospect because the call goes to voice mail. The question is, how do you deal with it?

Personally, I leave messages only occasionally, because I'm not a big fan of "one-way communication." When the person I've called hears the message, they can listen to what I've said without my being able to gauge their reaction, and without an indication of interest there is little I can do. Then, when I go to follow up the call, I am faced with a person whose opinion has already been formed, and perhaps negatively so.

If, however, after numerous calls you continue to get the voice mail, you will want to leave a message. If so, take the following points into consideration.

- Do not leave a spontaneous message. Better to hang up and call back later when you're well prepared.
- It helps to write down your message beforehand and rehearse it aloud a few times. Then proceed to call again.
- The message should be as brief as possible; it should not last more than 30 seconds.
- Don't give away too much information. Simply bait the hook.
- Get rid of all terms with "promotional" or "salesmanlike" overtones.

- Script structure: Who you are, the reason for your call and your "hook" (optional), contact details, and availability (optional)
- Speak in a calm, measured and clear voice, keep your sentences short and use a pleasant but firm tone. And smile!
- Record your message on your own voice mail, and hone it until you are satisfied with it (not only *what* you're saying, but above all, *how* you say it).

Version 1

"Good morning, Mr. Client, this is Ramon Hernandez. Since I wasn't able to reach you today, could you please call me back at your earliest convenience? My number is xxx-xxx-xxxx. Have a nice day."

It is precisely the brevity of the message, and the fact that you are withholding the reason for your call, that often ensures that your call is returned.

Version 2

"Good morning, Mr. Client, this is Ramon Hernandez with LogiSpeed. The reason I'm calling is that I need information concerning your logistics processes. Since you were not available today, could you please call me back briefly? You can reach me all day tomorrow at xxx-xxx-xxxx. Have a nice day."

Version 3

"Good morning, Mr. Client, this is Ramon Hernandez with LogiSpeed. Since you were not available today, could you please call me back? It concerns the optimization of your logistics processes through decentralized hubs. You can reach me all day tomorrow at xxx-xxx-xxxx. Have a nice day."

Keep in mind that your goal here is to obtain a call from the client. Therefore, you don't necessarily need to provide any more information than that. However, if you want more "flesh on the bones" . . .

Version 4
"Good morning, Mr. Client, this is Ramon Hernandez from LogiSpeed. I'd like to personally show you how you can boost your key performance indicators for logistics while lowering your overhead—but only if you think you can benefit from it. Please call me back in the course of the week and we can discuss your decision on the matter. From experience I can tell that this inquiry will only take 5 minutes of your time. I look forward to hearing from you. You can reach me all day tomorrow at xxx-xxx-xxxx. Have a nice day."

If you should not get a response, simply wait a few days and call again. By using the versions above, you have the option of "enriching" each follow-up message. In this way you don't come across as wooden, but genuinely enhance the value of your call—and this boosts your response rate in turn.

If you like, for your nth message you can use the approach below:

Version 5

"My wife thinks I'm crazy to be calling you yet again after having received no response from you yet . . . Good morning, Mr. Client, it's Ramon Hernandez from LogiSpeed. And if you're asking yourself, '(Why) should I call Ramon Hernandez back, then I'd just like to tell you that I would never dare phone you this many times if I wasn't 100% certain that I have something to offer you. Something that will make your job as head of logistics easier and more effective. That's a promise, and you can hold me to it. I look forward to hearing from you. You can reach me all day tomorrow at xxx-xxx-xxxx. Have a nice day."

Summary:

- Starting with a proper greeting (in content, structure, articulation, and tone) you are laying the foundation for a successful call.

- If you don't get the information you need from the switchboard, try the sales department.

- See the gatekeepers for what they are: people. Therefore, treat them accordingly with respect.

- By using new and effective techniques with the PA, you significantly increase your success rate—and the same goes for your voice mail messages.

5
How to Win Over the Decision Maker

In this chapter you will be shown special conversational gambits that will make you significantly more successful in your cold calls with decision makers. The following openers are surprisingly easy. At the same time they are enormously effective, because they don't even begin to trigger the prospect's defense mechanism. Rather they lure her into discussion.

The end result is that she will be happy to speak with you. Even the more difficult conversations — which until now were over shortly after they had begun — you'll find yourself able to sustain and direct on your terms.

As we discussed in chapter 2, we often do precisely that which leads to what we fear most: failure. By

reverting to the old textbook patterns we are usually the
ones who provoke rejection from the client. Let's put an
end to that right now.

5.1 New and Effective Openers That Are Guaranteed to Work

It is important to create a pleasant mood right from
the start. The foundation for this will be your clear and
articulate greeting and friendly tone of voice, followed by
a brief pause to allow the client to return the gesture. This
is what establishes a dialogue in the first few seconds.

And now the question is: How do you capture the
interest and attention of your prospect and direct it
through the conversation and toward your goal?

Straight to the point

"I have no time!" is the most dreaded of all customer
reactions. Do you get that too? In that case I have an
opener for you which will prevent you from hearing
that reaction ever again. In fact, you will now hear the
prospect say, "Yes, of course." In other words, you will
be getting the consent of the customer and triggering a
positive emotion. And all of that precisely at the juncture
at which you used to hear "I have no time!" You're
probably thinking, "Is that even possible?" Let's see.

Imagine what is going through the mind of a customer
when he gets a cold call: Decision makers in particular,

and people who are generally very busy, do not like it when a caller talks too much and doesn't get to the point. They get impatient because they have no desire to waste their precious time with calls of this nature.

From now on, always use the following opener in your cold calls. You will set yourself refreshingly apart from the rest of the pack and will get the immediate attention and consent from people who truly feel they have no time to spare:

Hernandez: "Good morning, Mr. Baley, this is Ramon Hernandez from LogiSpeed. How are you doing?"
Pause.
Head of Logistics: "Good morning."
Hernandez: "Mr. Baley, may I get straight to the point?"
HL: "Yes, of course."

99% of the time, using the opener "May I get straight to the point?" will reward you with a "Yes, please," "Yes, of course" or something similar. You have my word on that. And you will be stunned the first time you experience it on the phone.

It is crucial that you do not hesitate or speak in an uncertain manner, but rather that you take the lead both in the content of your offer and the tone of your voice.

Use this opener consistently following your greeting, and you will get the immediate attention of your prospect and a receptive reaction. From now on, *prior* to every cold call you make, you can rest easy in the knowledge that you will get the consent of the client and trigger a positive emotion. Simple, yet powerful, isn't it?

The *straight-to-the-point technique* also offers another decisive advantage. Reread the script above and take notice: There is a double exchange occurring.

This twofold exchange in the initial seconds is paramount, precisely because most other prospectors reel off their script without pausing, causing the client to lose interest instantly and stonewall the caller. With the *straight-to-the-point technique* you disarm the prospect, breaking his reaction patterns and actively engaging him from the outset. The result is a very natural exchange between two people.

The anticipation technique

This method is highly effective if you're working in an industry in which the customer already has a partner for the product you are proposing. In this case, the objection "We're already set, thank you" in all its variations is practically the rule.

The *anticipation technique* as a conversational gambit is also a good choice, if you are frequently faced with a specific objection.

The rule here is simple: The best objection is one that is never raised. Therefore, take the objection away from your prospect by raising it yourself first. In this manner you get a yes and his consent and will be able to break through sticking points which used to hamper your calls and would often spell the end of the exchange:

Hernandez: "Mr. Baley, may I get straight to the point?"
HL: "Yes, of course."
Hernandez: "I'm assuming you already have a logistics partner, correct?"
HL: "Indeed, I do."

By means of this small shift, the quality of your conversations will make a 180-degree turn for the better. Whereas before, the phrase "We're already set, thank you" signaled the end of the call, now you will get a yes and can continue your conversation seamlessly:

Hernandez: "Great, then you're exactly the person I'm looking for. If there's *one* thing in the area of Asian freight shipping about which you would say, 'If you can solve that, then I'm interested?,' what would that be? What comes to mind?"
Or,
Hernandez: "Great, that's the reason I'm calling you today. It is precisely companies like yours with existing partners that use us as an *additional* partner, for specific logistics issues. What are the particular challenges that you face in the area of logistics?"

The *anticipation technique* can of course be used for any desired and anticipated objection.

The ultimate pattern breaker

This kind of opener is a particular one. Why?

With this method you avoid saying anything that the client may have already heard. In other words, you will use openers that differ so drastically from the norm, that you will draw laughs from your prospect. Before you know it you've broken the ice and you can carry on in a fresh and favorable manner. As a wise man once said, "A client's smile and a yes are your road to success." The *ultimate pattern breaker* is the only technique which doesn't adhere to any fixed structure; it's your creativity that is called for here!

In order to get you started on your own versions of this method, below are some examples. These *pattern breakers* were developed together with my seminar participants and have proven themselves in the field. Make sure to use a jovial tone with these openers. And a smile can never hurt . . .

Hernandez: "Good morning, Mr. Baley, this is Ramon Hernandez with LogiSpeed. How are you?" Pause.

HL: "Good morning."

Hernandez: "Mr. Baley, may I get straight to the point?"

HL: "Of course you may."

Hernandez: "I'm on a search for new customers and thought of you!"

One thing is clear when using this approach: You have to trust yourself, and what you say has to suit your temperament. I often hear my seminar participants say, "I cannot imagine how this would work with any serious decision maker . . . It doesn't sound very businesslike!" But only a few weeks later, I hear these same people say, "It's incredible, the pattern breakers work great—and they're fun, for me and my customer! I would never have thought so."

Let's look at some further examples:

You: "Normally cold calling is not really my thing, but for you, Ms. Client, I just had to make an exception . . ."

Or,

You: "I'm certain that a year from now you'll be saying, 'Ramon, you are the best logistics partner for Asian freight shipping!' Ms. Client, what would allow you to actually say this in a year's time?"

Or,

You: "Ms. Client, for the next 2 minutes and 11 seconds I'd like to discuss (your subject), is that OK?"

My advice is to take a chance, try it out and look forward to your customer's reaction. You'll surprise your prospect with such humor that often she won't have a choice but to smile, or better, to laugh in acknowledgment of your effort.

The TT special

My goal was to go beyond all the above-mentioned techniques and develop something so innovative that it would work regardless of the industry or the prospect in question. It took two years and hundreds of prospecting calls to hone the following method. And now, like a master key, it opens nearly all possible doors. That has made the technique my personal favorite.

The TT special derives its power from the fact that it addresses exactly those questions which every prospect unconsciously asks himself. And what would you say those questions are?

1. Who is this?
2. What does he want?
3. How long is this going to take?
4. Does he have my interests at heart?
   (Or does he just want to sell me something?)
5. What am I getting out of this?

Because many prospectors leave one or more of these questions unanswered in their opening, these unanswered questions begin to surface from the unconscious into the conscious mind of the client. And the moment they do, the client becomes impatient, and in turn, loses interest. If you are able to answer questions 1 through 5 in your opening, the prospect will remain interested in what you have to say.

The TT special adheres to the following structure:
- Establish your thematic focus.
- State what you're after.
- Let the customer feel that the decision is his to make.
- Stay in control of the conversation through questions.

In practice, this is what it looks like:

Hernandez: "Good morning, Mr. Baley, this is Ramon Hernandez from LogiSpeed. How are you doing?"

HL: "Good morning."

Hernandez: "Mr. Baley, may I get straight to the point?"

HL: "Of course."

Hernandez: "Regarding the optimization of your Asian freight shipments I'd like to meet with you personally — but only if you think you can benefit from it. To decide whether you can, I have a brief question, is that OK?"

HL: "Uh . . . OK"

Or,

Hernandez: "Mr. Baley, may I get straight to the point?"

HL: "Of course."

Hernandez: "We would like to become your additional strategic logistics partner — but only if we could benefit mutually from it. That's why I have a brief question, OK?"

HL: "Er . . . alright."

Please note that the last word preceding the "but" (". . . to meet with you personally — *but only* . . ." — in this case the word "personally") should be spoken in practically the same breath as the "but only." It is *after* the "only" (emphasize this word!) that there should be a slight pause. In this way you will maximize its effect.

Try to adhere firmly to the overall structures shown above. The specifics of content, however, can and should be varied, as with all of the techniques illustrated in this book. It is the underlying structure which remains the same. This particular opening technique outlined above, then, will be your key to all customer doors. Good luck!

5.2 Investigating the Customer's Needs: Persuasion Without Argumentation

Through your skillful opening you have, in turn, "opened up" the prospect, so that she is ready to engage in a dialogue with you. With targeted questions (customer needs assessment) it is necessary to find out:

- What aspects of your field and your offer are important to your client?
- What can motivate your client to make an appointment?

The needs assessment is one of the most important phases in cold calling, and is precisely the aspect most often neglected or left out completely by many prospectors. Most callers spend too much time talking about themselves and their offer, as opposed to engaging the customer with targeted questions, putting the focus on her and giving her the lion's share of talking time. Consequently, the customer senses that the caller merely wants to sell her something, in other words, that he is more interested in himself and his deal than in her, her opinion or the best solution for her business. The end result is a high rate of rejection and a low rate of success, which is only natural because nobody welcomes that style of selling anymore.

That is why our thinking in sales nowadays is: Replace more and more of your statements with questions.

We can only persuade and win over the client once we have established and understood his decision criteria. So how do we find out what makes the customer tick?

Exactly, by asking questions. Structured and targeted questions.

In my opinion this is the paramount skill required in sales to begin with: Become adept at posing questions. Those who master questions master prospecting.

In the following pages I will provide you with new, concrete approaches, so that you can succeed in what appears to be an impossible task: You will persuade without resorting to argumentation — and thereby reach your objective much more easily than you have in the past.

So that you can work with targeted questions in a more natural and consistent manner, we are going to look at the tangible advantages of this approach for your prospecting success. Here are seven good reasons you should be working more frequently with questions:

1. The pull effect: You draw the client into the conversation.

2. Those who ask the question control the discussion, and controlling the discussion is the essence of prospecting.
3. The customer senses when you're genuinely interested, and this boosts his receptiveness in a profound way.
4. You increase the talking time of your client: International studies have found that in successful prospecting conversations the customer's talking time was at least 70%.
5. The client discovers what he really wants: With targeted questions you trigger a thought process which can lead to a realization on the part of the client.
6. You understand more of your customer's business world and are given sales opportunities. In other words, through the answers you receive from the customer, you obtain concrete "access points" to make an appointment or close the deal.
7. Assumptions narrow the mind, questions unlock it.

The TAXIS method

Time and again during my years as an employee in the manufacturing as well as the service industry, I asked a particular question in my cold calling which consistently (!) yielded powerful results. The prospect opened up and revealed those aspects which were crucial to my success: his desires and decision criteria. Decision criteria are simply those criteria on which the client makes his decisions (e.g. whether or not to make an appointment).

When I became independent as a sales trainer years ago, I developed a model based on this concept, which generated four simple and effective questions, forming the *TAXIS method*. The aim of this method is to look into the heart and mind of your customer.

Given that the *TAXIS method* was a product of experience and designed for concrete use—and is successfully employed in a variety of industries—I recommend that you incorporate it directly into your repertoire. Let yourself be surprised at how much easier it will be to engage the client in discussion. Your prospect will name her decision criteria for you. You will gain access to subtle background information and will practically be able to read her thoughts. Think about it for a moment: What would it mean to you to be able to effortlessly access the decision criteria of your customer in any given cold call?

The four questions of the *TAXIS method*

So, if you can't actually read thoughts . . . give the *TAXIS method* a try. It should be applied directly following your opening. Before we go into the details of the method and see how it can be incorporated into your script, let's have a look at the questions themselves in their basic form:

"Mr. Client, when you think about your (challenges/ desires),
1. what is important to you in this regard, what matters to you most?
2. . . . and what else?

3. Which aspect is the most important?
4. And beyond the points you've mentioned, Mr. Client, what is it that you personally feel strongly about?

Introduction: "When you think about your (challenges/desires) . . ."
With this introduction you establish your thematic focus. You're leading the client directly to the theme which you are looking to discuss. It is crucial that you establish this focus clearly and precisely.

Question 1: "What is important to you in this regard, what matters to you most?"
The first question bears directly on the desires and decision criteria of your client. It is vital that you start with open-ended questions and that you ask two of them: " . . . what is important to you in this regard, what matters to you most?"

Through this deliberate doubling of the question, the inquiry creates a heightened pull effect. The customer will open up to you. And that is exactly what you need: a customer who is happy to speak with you.

When using these questions, and all other questions in this book, feel free to use a wording that suits you personally.

People will rarely express everything they have to say with the first question they are asked. That is in part because they don't automatically think of all aspects at once. It is also because they don't have a conscious, structured list of criteria in mind at that very moment. That is why the second question is just as important.

Question 2: "And what else is important to you?"
Make sure you pose this second question as an open-ended question, too. Don't ask, "Is that all?" but "*What else* is important to you?"

Please note: The *TAXIS method* is highly effective for investigating all of your customer's decision criteria in a concrete manner. However, when aiming for an appointment on the first contact with a client, not all of the decision criteria are necessary. The benefit of the *TAXIS method* for cold calling is above all that the client is sharing this information with you.

In most cases, asking the first question (which is, in fact, two questions) will suffice for a successful cold call.

Through the answers you receive from the customer, you will be able to spot concrete openings for proposing an appointment, and move directly to a successful conclusion.

Later, when meeting your customer face-to-face or when selling on the phone, it is best to use all four questions.

When you do decide to employ all four questions (e.g. when meeting face-to-face), be aware that after the second question you still won't know all the forces driving your client's decisions. That is why it would be beneficial to pose this second question again. In fact, repeat the second question of the *TAXIS method* until you feel that "Alright, now he's told me everything." However, be sure to alter the wording each successive time; you don't want to sound like a broken record. For example: "Beyond that, what do yo value highly?" or "What else do you aspire to?"

This requires a subtle feel for communication. The client should neither feel under interrogation, nor become impatient.

Question 3: "Of the points A, B, C that you've mentioned (repeat them!), Mr. Client, what would be at the top of your list?"

Why is the assessment of the client's priority relevant here? Because you learn where his main focus lies and can then adapt your own focus in your argumentation or offer accordingly.

Until now you've spoken to your customer about his *business* decision criteria.

Question 4: This question goes beyond the business realm and targets the *personal* criteria of the customer, aiming to establish the principle of personal benefit:

"Mr. Client, a final question for you personally: Apart from the criteria you mentioned, what do you *personally* feel strongly about?"

A sensitive question, certainly, but a crucial one. Why? Commercial benefit determines *what* a client buys. Personal benefit determines *why he is buying from you*. Therefore, if you can identify the personal aspirations of the client, then you have the highest possible chances of reaching your goal. That is also why this question is a special one: It requires exceptional communicative skill.

Integrating the *TAXIS method* into your script

Now we will look at how to incorporate the *TAXIS method* into the flow of the conversation (we will again take up the example of Mr. Hernandez who is trying to make an appointment with the head of logistics of the wholesale firm Carter & Sons):

Hernandez: "Good morning, Mr. Baley, this is Ramon Hernandez with LogiSpeed. How are you doing?"

HL: "Good morning."

Hernandez: "Mr. Baley, may I get straight to the point?"

HL: "Yes, please."

Hernandez: "We would like to become your additional logistics partner—but only if it would be mutually beneficial. I'd like to ask you a brief question on the matter, is that alright?"

HL: "Well, OK . . ."

Hernandez: "If you imagine working with an additional logistics partner, what profile would that partner need to have, what matters to you most in concrete terms?"

The following variation is most effective when you're faced with a particularly tough customer.

Example of the *TAXIS method* applied to a specific aspect:

Hernandez: "I'd like to meet with you to discuss the optimization of your Asian freight shipping — but only if you think you could benefit from it. To decide whether you can, I have a brief question, is that alright?"

HL: "Um, OK, go ahead . . ."

Hernandez: "If you could name *one* thing in the area of Asian freight shipping that doesn't run as smoothly as you would like, what *one* thing would that be? What comes to mind?"

In practice, you will discover how naturally the customers share this information. In this kind of approach in which you are not babbling on about yourself ("We are a company that . . . we make . . . we do . . .," etc.) but rather focusing on the client with targeted questions, the quality of your calls will move significantly from a push to a pull. In other words, you will no longer be overselling, but drawing the client to you. This will render your prospecting venture much more pleasant and much easier — for you and your client.

The best part about this technique is that in most cases, when using the *TAXIS method* you will no longer need any argumentation. It sounds far-fetched, but it's true. The reason is that there is a psychological mechanism by which a person who guides another person mentally through their desires and needs will be seen as the one holding the key to those very desires and needs. The prospect will unconsciously yield to this process. This principle is very effective in the field, and is what I call "persuasion without argumentation."

Through the answers of the customers you will be given direct opportunities to make your appointment and — without argumentation — to conclude a successful call.

Hernandez: "If there's *one* thing in the area of Asian freight shipping that doesn't run as smoothly as you would like, what *one* thing would that be? Off the top of your head?

HL: "Well, there is the issue of the hubs. Our partners sometimes have prolonged delivery times, because everything goes through the main loading stations — that means that things don't always go 100% according to plan . . ."

Hernandez: "I see. What would you want to see done in concrete terms?"

HL: "It's simple: We'd like to see shorter delivery times by means of decentralized processes."

Hernandez: "That is the reason I'm calling you today: With us as partners you can attain shorter delivery times through decentralized processes. What I propose is that you get an idea of what this would look like for your company. What day would suit you best to meet next week?"

HL: "Mmm, let's make it Tuesday morning at 9 o'clock then, alright?"

I urge you to try this out. It's a wonderful approach.

Your customers will feel valued and understood. This is how prospecting can be fun, by raising the quality and, above all, lending more depth to the exchange, with direct benefits to your success rate.

Admittedly, things don't always go smoothly; we get objections on the phone too. In chapter 5.4, we will see how to handle these effectively.

Concrete tips for the application of the *TAXIS method*

- It is not about the questions you ask, but the answers you get from the client. Therefore, actively listen and consistently take note of his criteria.
- You are not a question-dispensing robot, but a person speaking with another person. Therefore, allow yourself to react genuinely, using natural fillers between one answer and the next question such as, "Yes, that's a good point . . . and beyond that, what else strikes you personally as important?"
- By using additional questions, flesh out statements from the customer that may be a little too vague, for example: "Of course, I understand. In that case, what are you seeking in practical terms?"
- Periodically recap the client's stated criteria verbatim. In this way you'll forge a more genuine understanding between yourself and the client.
- List all of the customer's criteria. Only then should you proceed to argue your point (if need be).
- In order to set an appointment, the first set of questions is usually all you will need.

5.3 Client-Centered Argumentation

Client-centered argumentation is a core competency in sales. "Benefit statement" would be a more traditional term for it. I, however, have chosen to call it "client-centered argumentation" because it expresses more precisely what it's about: a shift in perspective in the benefit statement. It is not we or our product that are the focal points, but whatever benefits the customer. It is the customer's perspective that counts.

As we have mentioned, in most cases where the aim is a "qualified appointment," there is no need for lengthy argumentation. You are not required to sell the customer on your company or your product—and you shouldn't.

Don't shoot your bolt on the phone. Rather, you should try to create an arc of suspense leading up to your appointment.

However, because many salespeople jump into their pitch even before the client has "settled into the conversation," let alone expressed what is important to her, many prospecting calls remain unsuccessful.

I urge you to do it differently: Give the customer exactly (and only) what she wants to hear! That is to say, ask her before you bring your arguments to bear. As soon as you know what is important to her and what her decision criteria are, you can home in on the benefits you are bringing with a few well-chosen, specific and concrete arguments.

It makes no difference what your product can or can't do. The only thing that makes a difference is what you bring to the client *from her perspective.*

The motto here should be: What counts is not *what* we do, but *what it does for the customer.*

And they need to understand this! So it is up to us as sales professionals to convey this to each and every customer.

If you succeed in conveying the benefit you bring to the client from her perspective and in her own words, then you've won. Why? Because the client will never raise objections to her own words. Therefore, make the shift in perspective when stating the benefits—you will give yourself the best possible chance of success.

Now we're going to look at exactly how this is done:

The feature/advantage/benefit distinction

Oftentimes we confuse features and advantages with benefits. And particularly when we are convinced of our products or services, or we are experts in our field, we tend to proudly showcase the features and refinements of our product. There is only one thing, however, that interests the customer. It is the concrete and specific answer to the question: "What does this do for me?" Thus, it isn't the products and their features and advantages which count, but only the practical benefit— from the customer's personal perspective.

Features

Features are the characteristics, the elements that make up a product. These can include its lifespan, its performance/function, its ease of handling, its integration in existing processes, etc. Features have a purely descriptive character. For example:

"I offer practical prospecting training sessions, in which you will learn to apply new techniques based on real-life scenarios from your business."

Does that sound like a benefit to you? In fact, it is only a *description* of my product.

Advantages

Advantages illustrate to what extent the features of a product *can* be of help to a customer. Arguments which present a product's advantages speak in general terms. They *can* be arguments of benefit, but only if the customer has expressed a desire for precisely *that* advantage.

Take this example:

"You will see a direct and quantifiable gain by taking part in my training sessions."

Benefit

A benefit is always concrete, tangible and tailored to the individual. That is what distinguishes it from an advantage. The benefit reveals the value of a product's advantages, that is to say, how your solution will help the client in practical terms. It is on this argumentation level that you will be most successful.

In order to effectively employ benefit statements, it is indispensable to find out the client's decision criteria, her desires, and her needs—that is, *before* you begin your argumentation! Say, for instance, that a client wants her sales team to double their success rate in cold calling:

"After the training sessions, your salespeople will double their success rate on the phone."

Practical tips for client-centered argumentation

From my experience I can tell you that when using the client-centered approach, it is easiest if you follow the structure below in four distinct steps:

1. Repetition of the customer's goals
2. Use the formulation: "Because we . . . + feature/advantage of your product/service"
3. "In concrete terms, for you this means that . . . + benefit of your product/service"
4. A closed and concluding question, such as, "Is this what you are looking to accomplish?"

Example:

(. . .)

Hernandez: "If there is *one* thing in the area of Asian freight shipping that is not running as smoothly as you would want from a logistics perspective, what would you say that *one* thing is? What comes to mind?"

HL: "Well, OK, there is the issue of the hubs; our partners occasionally have longer delivery times, due to the fact that everything runs through the main loading stations. This is not always 100% to our liking . . ."

Hernandez: "I can understand that. What would you like to see happen in practical terms?"

HL: "Simple: shorter delivery times through decentralized processes!

Hernandez: "That is precisely the reason for my call today: With us as partners you'll be able to attain shorter delivery times through decentralized processes. What I propose is that you get an idea of what this would look like for your company. What day of next week would it be convenient for you to meet?"

HL: "Not so fast . . . I need to know more about it before I can determine that it's worth making an appointment. You'll have to be a little clearer as to whether it makes sense for me."

Hernandez (laughs): "Naturally, what you're after is shorter delivery times through decentralized processes . . . and because we don't work through one exclusive hub, but have a loading station in every country, for you this means being able to accelerate delivery through decentralized processes. Would that meet your needs?"

HL: "Yes, it would."

Hernandez: "Great. In that case, Mr. Baley, when would it suit you best to meet so that we can discuss how this would work for you in concrete terms?"

HL: "Hmm, let's say Tuesday morning, 9 o'clock, alright?"

Why is this client-oriented line of reasoning so effective?

1. Because you're asking questions *before* invoking arguments.
2. Because you are feeding back the benefits to the client in his own words. And he will find it hard to object to his own assertions . . .

Test this approach out, and you will see how effortlessly it works in your calls.

5.4 "No Time, Not Interested, Please Send Us Your Details": How to Handle These Objections Skillfully

Let me get straight to the point: If you apply these methods to handle objections, your success rate will skyrocket. Conversations which used to founder on objections you will now be able to conduct on your own terms.

The effectiveness of these techniques will give you such security and self-confidence that you will be all but impervious to objections, for no customer wakes up in the morning and starts thinking up new objections out of the blue. It is always the same objections we are faced with on the phone . . .

Objection handling: What to pay attention to

Dealing with objections in a professional manner is one of the biggest challenges in sales and prospecting. Why? Because they undermine our confidence. But again, it doesn't have to be this way. If you're willing to take the time to prepare yourself *once*, but professionally, you will be armed for life. From now on you will know exactly what to say in order to continue the conversation in a smooth and charming manner. And always keep in mind that the objections you face are few and always the same ones.

If the customer weighs the pros and cons in a rational manner and then says no, her objection is a factual one. It is a tangible objection based on content and facts which must be analyzed and solved.

Most of the objections in cold calling, however, are on a relationship level: The prospect doesn't even begin to engage with us on the content of our offer because she's in no mood for a cold call and immediately shuts down. In this case, we are not dealing with a genuine objection but a pretext.

In terms of our approach, however, it doesn't do us much good to distinguish between an objection and a pretext, because we will still have to effectively deal with anything our customer throws at us.

Remember that many prospectors approach their calls using outdated patterns that no one wants to hear, and thereby trigger the rejection mechanism of the client. Simply put, most objections are provoked by the prospector himself! The methods laid out in this book will put an end to that. From now on you will hear much fewer objections than ever before.

The prevalent opinion amongst sales trainers is that the goal of objection handling is to convince the client of the opposite of his present opinion. According to them, the client requires a trenchant (counter-)argument to his objection. But this approach is ineffective and often even counterproductive. Why? The law of nature states: For every instance of pressure, there is an equal and opposite counter-pressure.

When a customer raises an objection, for example, "Not interested," we usually perceive this as a kind of pressure. Then when we react with a "Yes, but . . ." or begin to argue our case, saying, "But we have an innovative product that . . ." And this creates a counter-pressure.

The consequence is that the game of pressure/counter-pressure only worsens, until someone gives up or is cut off. And usually it's not the client but the prospector. In short, this doesn't work. So how does it work?

The real goal of handling an objection is *to stay in the conversation*. Or rather, to parry the objection and come back in a smooth manner — exactly at those junctures where the client is trying to get you off the line. And in that situation, it isn't arguments that will help you, but disarming questions.

The rule here is: Objections thrive on (counter-)arguments, but are silenced with understanding and questions which foster communication.

Notorious objections and how to handle them
Have you ever taken the time to reflect on and note down the objections that you hear most when cold calling? People rarely do this. If, however, we list all the objections we encounter, commit them to memory and prepare ourselves for them, we will have the ideal weapons to overcome them.

That's why we're going to look at the preparation together. Please take a few minutes to list all the objections you can recall hearing from your clients during cold calls, then read on.

There, now you have all of your clients' objections clearly before you. There isn't much variety in them, is there?

In the following pages we will look at all the classic objections and the most effective means of dealing with them. Here again it is vital that you remain true to yourself. I will provide you with a few variations in each case, so that you can select the one that suits you best.

Feel free to get creative and come up with your own formulations.

There are two additional aspects that I find crucial to this process. The first is: Approach the handling of objections in a playful manner! Mix and match the techniques that are illustrated here. They can be very easily combined. The second point is: Show "sportsmanship" when handling objections. If you've received three objections, dealt with each and made it back into the conversation, and the customer suddenly raises a fourth, then you can bow out of the call in a friendly manner. Handling three objections — if they should arise — should in my opinion be a requirement for us as prospectors.

In reality, most prospectors unfortunately give in after the first objection. If you use the following techniques consistently, this will not be your case in the future!

Let's now look at the different kinds of objections in detail.

The classics

As a sales trainer, every week I meet with many people who work in B2B sales. Regardless of the industry we're talking about, it is always the same objections that we come across in prospecting. Here are the ones heard most often:

- The time objection: "I have no time at the moment."
- The regular supplier objection: "We're satisfied with our present supplier."
- The details objection: "Please send me your details."

- The no-need objection: "We have no need at the moment."
- The no-interest objection: "I'm not interested."

Even if not all the objections you've noted down figure in this list, I can assure you that the techniques you are about to learn here will be easily applicable to any further variations that you might encounter.

Direct application: How the techniques work in practice

First I will present the techniques individually, then we will move into the practical application with reference to each objection in question.

The anticipation technique

This technique is simple: You raise the client's potential objection yourself and thereby deliberately disarm the client. So that the client doesn't beat you to the objection, you will have to bring it up already in your opening. That is why I addressed this method in chapter 5.1.

The *anticipation technique* is the only *proactive* objection-handling method. We are acting instead of reacting.

However, in all cases in which it is the customer who raises the objection first, the following structure is the most effective way to handle it:

1. The customer raises an objection.
2. You deflect the objection.
3. You open up the customer through questions.

Conditional consent
Here it is the principle of "deflecting pressure" which comes into play. In other words: Be like water, not like rock, and yield to adversity instead of resisting it . . .

Do not resist the force of an objection, but deflect it first. Customers are used to meeting resistance. If you reverse the trend and show understanding and acceptance in the future, the customer will subconsciously remain receptive. Conditional consent means that you are not fully agreeing with the customer, but doing so on a relationship level (respecting the person and her opinion). Factually (on a content level), you are not agreeing.

ALWAYS use this technique, before resorting to any of the following.

The counter-question
This technique is as easy as its name implies: You counter an objection with a question. By using a question you are opening the client up, persuading him to share his opinion and giving yourself a way back into the conversation.

Use the following methods consistently! You will remain in the conversation and/or find your way back into it if required.

The time objection: "I have no time."

In many industries, this is the most notorious objection. As far as you are concerned, this can now be a part of the past. Surely you've read chapter 5.1 and figured out how to do this. After the greeting, apply the following technique:

Straight to the point
   Client: "Derek Baley speaking."
   You: "Good morning, Mr. Baley, this is Ramon Hernandez from LogiSpeed. How are you doing?"
   Client: "Good morning."
   You: "Mr. Baley, may I get straight to the point?"
   Client: "Yes, of course."

The prospect will always answer "Yes, of course" (or similar) when greeted with this opener. In other words, you will even get a positive response from the customer! This will do wonders for your confidence and mindset. It is just a great feeling knowing that from now on you will be getting a yes and a friendly reaction at the outset of every cold call.

The regular supplier objection: "We're satisfied with our present supplier."

This objection in all its guises is also a classic. In chapter 5.1 you already learned of an effective way around this:

The anticipation technique

You: "Mr. Baley, may I get straight to the point?"

Client: "Yes, of course."

You: "I'm assuming that you already have a logistics partner, correct?"

Client: "Naturally."

At this juncture you have different options which were discussed in chapter 5.1.

Conditional consent

Rule: Yield to adversity.

This is the first "reactive" technique, that is to say, when the customer raises an objection in the course of a call and we must react to it:

Client: "Thank you, but we're satisfied with the logistics suppliers that we have!"

You: "Uh-huh, I see."

That's the short version. Simple as that.

The longer version might sound like this:

You: "I see, especially in a vital area like logistics it's important to have reliable partners."

In both cases you're deflecting the force of the objection and showing consideration. Your customer senses that you're not looking to attack. He will increasingly let down his guard and be more receptive. If you take advantage of this and proceed to ask targeted questions, you will usually be rewarded with answers. And just like that, you're back in the game.

Important: Apply the *conditional consent technique* ALWAYS as a first reaction to a client's objection. And from there carry on seamlessly. This method cannot stand alone; you must keep the momentum going in your favor. To do this, follow it up with this:

The counter-question

Client: "Thank you, but we're satisfied with the logistics suppliers that we have!"

You: "I see. In terms of logistics and especially sensitive processes, what is essential for you? What matters to you most?"

By now you'll be familiar with this structure: It's the *TAXIS method* (see chapter 5.2). It is especially effective in cold calling. Through the doubling of open questions regarding the desires of the client, you exert a pull effect and draw the client's attention back into the exchange. You will be surprised at how naturally you will now get answers from you client.

Variation 1

You: "That's great to hear. It is precisely companies like yours with existing partners that use us as additional partners when dealing with special challenges and sensitive processes: What would you say are your special challenges? What areas do you find gaining importance in the future?"

Variation 2 – The ace up your sleeve

Let's say the customer reacts with a "No, we're

satisfied with our suppliers" to both alternatives above — which rarely happens — then the following turbo technique is *guaranteed* to get you through, no matter how tough the customer may be:

You: "Mr. Customer, in that case I just have one final question, is that OK?"

Every customer faced with this question will think, "OK" and say, "Alright, go ahead." In this way you'll come back from the brink in the toughest situations.

Example:

Client: "No, we're very satisfied with our present suppliers, as I said before."

You: "That's fine, Mr. Customer, in that case I have one final question, is that alright?"

Client: "OK."

You: "If you could name *one* aspect in the area of logistics that is most pressing to you, what would that be? What *single* aspect would you like to improve?"

By zeroing in on a very specific aspect, the *TAXIS method* exerts an even more compelling effect in extreme situations. Always remember to double your questions! The vast majority of customers will respond to this, and you'll be back in the conversation.

The details objection: "Send us your details first."
There will be clients, although very few, who really want to inform themselves before consenting to an appointment or sending us an inquiry. In the majority of cases, "Send us your details first" or "Send us a

proposal" (the latter usually without a prolonged discussion) is nothing more than a pretext! The clients know from experience that with this response they'll be rid of us more easily.

If it's our goal to make an appointment, then we will have failed if we simply agree to send over some details or a proposal. Moreover, we'll be wasting precious time sending material and following up with a client who is really not interested.

Conditional consent

    Client: "Send us your details first."

    You: "I understand."

    Or,

    You: "Oh, of course, you want to be better informed."

    That's the longer version.

    Then you can segue straight into the following:

The counter-question

    Client: "Send us your details first."

    You: "Of course, I understand that you want to be better informed. So that I can send you exactly the details that would really interest you, I have one final question, is that OK?"

    Client: "Go ahead . . ."

    You: "With respect to your Asian logistics processes, what is essential to you? What do you think could facilitate them in concrete terms?"

    Or,

    You: "If there is *one* aspect in the area of logistics that you find most pressing, what would that be? What *single* aspect would you want to improve?"

As you can see, the principle underlying these methods is a simple one. And before you know it, you're back in an engaging and professional exchange and can move decisively toward a successful conclusion with the aid of the answers you've garnered from the client.

A further variation:

Client: "Send us some details first."

You: "Of course. Mr. Client, I can tell that you would like to be better informed about my offer before we meet. But if you're asking for details out of politeness and are actually not interested, then feel free to say so. That's alright!"

What do you think of that? Perhaps you don't like it because you think you'll be dumped on the spot? In my view, it is better to immediately spot someone who is going to make you tread water and move on to the next call which might prove more profitable, than to toil away where you know you have no chance. In fact, about 50% of clients respond in the following manner:

Client: "Well, you know, we get so many calls from people here . . . if I were to meet with them all, I wouldn't get anything done."

You: "I can appreciate that, Mr. Client. In that case I have one final question, is that OK?"

Client: "Alright, go ahead."

You: "With regard to your Asian logistics processes, what would you have to hear from a discussion with us in practical terms, for you to say, 'If you can do that, then I want to see it'? What comes to mind?"

The no-need objection: "We have no need at the moment."

You must hear this objection pretty often, right? This is how to deal with these skillfully in the future:

The anticipation technique combined with the pattern breaker

You: "Mr. Client, I'm assuming that my call alone is not enough to trigger a need for additional logistics services, am I right?"

You will see that by using this approach you will readily break the ice and lighten the discussion. I would recommend following this up with the *TT special* (see chapter 5.1).

The counter-question with a twist

Client: "We have no need."

You: "I see. When you say 'no need,' is it because you're already well supplied or because you are not active in this area?"

Now you'll get one of two answers. If she says "We've got our suppliers," then go ahead with the variations mentioned above. If she says, "It doesn't concern us for the moment," then do not ask when you can get back in touch with her. Keep your eye on the prize until you've reached your goal:

Client: "It doesn't concern us for the moment."

Variation1
You: "I see, you must currently have other priorities. What issues in logistics would you say are currently relevant to your company and are in need of solutions?"

Variation 2
You: "I understand. What is the *one* most relevant issue for you about which you would say, 'If you can solve this, I want to see it.'? What would that *one* issue be at the moment?"

As you can see, there are various ways of solving the situations you are presented with.

The no-interest objection: "I'm not interested."
You probably hear this as often as you hear "no need", correct? They are similar objections — and so are the ways to handle them:

When handling the no-interest objection, you can apply all the techniques that you did for the no-need one, almost verbatim.

In conclusion, another piece of advice: By now you know the objections that you come across in your cold calls. I suggest you make a list of these and begin to shape your ideal objection-handling strategies in an organized manner and in writing. That way you'll be perfectly armed for the rest of your career. Regardless of what the client says, you'll be prepared to react effectively — and will never again be caught off guard . . . just the opposite!

5.5 Closing: How to Get a Yes From Your Client

Now is the time: You've reached the business end of the call. Here it stands to reason that because you're looking to close, you should be leading the conversation straight toward your target.

By means of closing techniques you will steer the customer toward a clear decision and harvest the fruits of your labor.

By closing techniques we should understand all means that we employ on our own initiative to reach our cold calling objective. The objective could include: a qualified appointment, the client's commitment to send an inquiry, an order, etc.

Closing techniques are either questions—closed questions, after all we're looking for a straight answer from the client—or requests.

Examples:
You: "Alright, Mr. Client, then I propose that we meet next week and together we can get a better idea of how our solution would benefit your company. When would it suit you? Is Monday OK?"

Or,

You: "That's fine, then what I propose is that we meet tomorrow and I'll bring my details directly to you so that we can clear up any questions you may have."

Or,

You: "Now that we've cleared up your questions, would you like to do business?"

Recognizing and using the closing signals of the customer

Clients often send out signals of consent, in other words, signs that tell us that they are "ripe for closing." However, many salespeople overlook these signals. Therefore, pay close attention to what the client is saying and how she says it. Actively listen!

So that you can recognize closing signals on the phone, here is a list of the salient ones:

- Concrete questions from the client in response to what you have said, such as, "How exactly would that work?"
- Verbal agreement, such as, "interesting," "I see, yes."
- One of the most important and often overlooked signals: The client shares information with you and answers your questions.

Especially when the client begins the conversation in an aloof manner, raises objections but then proceeds to answer your questions, that is an unmistakable closing signal!

Bottom Line:
As soon as you get a closing signal, make sure you close!

This you can do in a pleasant manner:

Client: "How exactly would that work?

You: "Mr. Client, that is precisely why I am calling you today. In order to show you concretely how this would work, I'd like to meet with you personally. When would it suit you best to meet next week?"

Any additional argument at this point in the conversation is unnecessary, and might even be counterproductive. You're not selling anything over the phone; your goal is to make an appointment. It is at that appointment that you'll be able to discuss everything you need to discuss.

As mentioned, don't shoot your bolt on the phone. Build an arc of suspense toward the appointment, and the moment you get a concrete question from the client, aim to close immediately.

One thing is certain: As soon as you *can* close, do so.

Once you've closed, further argument will not get you any closer to your goal.

At this point there is only one thing left to do:

How to say goodbye in a professional manner

Let's assume your customer has given you the green light and you've reached your immediate objective. Now that the appointment is in the bag and you've concluded your conversation, it is important that the customer does not regret her decision once she puts the phone down. This is what is known as buyer's remorse. I'm sure you've experienced this as a consumer yourself. Buyer's remorse can lead to a subsequent cancellation. This is something you obviously want to prevent. The customer needs to come away feeling good and certain that she has made the right decision. In order to nourish this certainty, follow the structure below at the conclusion of your cold call:

1. Positive emotion
   You: "Great, Ms. Client, I look forward to our meeting on . . ."

2. Clarifying the next step
   You: "Following our call you'll be getting an email from me (in which I will outline the main points of our conversation). You'll find my contact details there as well. Should you have any further questions between now and the time we meet, don't hesitate to ask! Finally, could you please give me your email address?"

Make sure, of course, that you do exactly what you said you would in your parting statement. In that way you can trust that your client too will keep up her end of the bargain.

Summary:

- In most cases, we are the ones who trigger rejection from the client—by using all the dated textbook formulas of the sales person.

- Break with old patterns and apply fresh methods. You will thereby draw different reactions and boost your success rate.

- By replacing your statements with questions, you will get the client to share information and obtain key opportunities for closing.

- You will persuade without having to argue excessively.

- When the client raises objections, be like water, not like rock—yield to adversity instead of resisting it.

- Arguments narrow the mind, questions unlock it: Draw the client back into the exchange by using questions.

- The objections you are faced with are always the same ones and are few in number; so prepare yourself thoroughly and professionally for them.

- Use the client's own words to guide the conversation toward your objective, because remember: The client will never raise objections to his own words . . .

Cold calling can be simple and highly successful—and a lot of fun. For you and your client!

I wish you much success and even more enjoyment in your cold calling ventures!

I'd like to close with The 3 Golden Rules of the Tim Taxis Training Philosophy:
1) Deliberately choose positive thoughts.
2) Leave people in a better state than you found them.
3) Follow rules 1 and 2 every day.

About the Author

tt@tim-taxis.com

Tim Taxis is a sales expert, university lecturer, professional speaker, and bestselling author.

The MBA graduate has held a variety of sales positions in the manufacturing industry and in complex service companies for many years.

In 2007 he founded his company Tim Taxis Training and is today one of the most prominent sales trainers and speakers in German-speaking Europe.

He gives inspiring keynote speeches and presentations the world over in English or German. His clients include major corporations, medium-sized companies as well as international market leaders.

Tim lives in Munich, Germany.

Other Tim Taxis Media

Bestselling business book "Heiß auf Kaltakquise – So vervielfachen Sie Ihre Erfolgsquote am Telefon," Haufe, 2nd edition, 2013
ISBN: 978-3648019917
230 pages, €24.80
("Hot For Cold Calling – How to Boost Your Success Rate on the Phone", comprehensive guide)

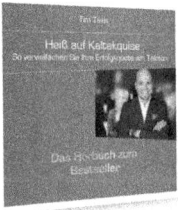

Audio "Heiß auf Kaltakquise"
RADIOROPA
EAN: 9783836807371
ASIN: B00FY41RWC
€19.95

Partner With Tim Taxis

If you are interested in publishing any of Tim's books or other media in English in the US or other countries, please contact Dr. Christiane Gierke at Tim's agency, text-ur copywriting and public relations agency
Dr. Gierke, at: info@text-ur.de

www.ingramcontent.com/pod-product-compliance
Lightning Source LLC
Chambersburg PA
CBHW071435210326
41597CB00020B/3802